Partakers

OF THE

DIVINE

**EXPERIENCING THE REALITY
OF CHRIST WITHIN...**

ISBN: **9781791682330**

PULPIT TO PAGE PUBLISHING CO. BOOKS MAY BE ORDERED THROUGH BOOKSELLERS OR BY CONTACTING:

PULPIT TO PAGE PUBLISHING CO.
WARSAW, INDIANA
PULPITTOPAGE.COM

Partakers

OF THE

DIVINE

EXPERIENCING THE REALITY
OF CHRIST WITHIN...

ALEX
PARKINSON

I would like to dedicate this, my first book, to my beautiful wife Jordan. You have been such a source of encouragement throughout the writing process. Listening to me read chapter after chapter, the Holy Spirit has used you to inspire as well as comfort and help. I love you deeply.

For further information on the ministry of

Alex & Jordan Parkinson and Mirror Image

Ministries Intl. visit:

web: a l e x p a r k i n s o n . o r g

facebook: A l e x & J o r d a n P a r k i n s o n

instagram: @ a l e x d p a r k i n s o n

youtube: A l e x P a r k i n s o n

I didn't want to put the book down! This is a great read. In providing his own personal battles Alex disempowers that personal monkey on everyone's back, that says, 'You are not qualified to minister because of any physical issue you may be carrying.' I really love the way he has openly woven his own story together with practical kingdom truth that is tried and tested. You will not only come away with a deeper desire for intimacy with God, but you will also receive essential keys to see Him manifest the kingdom in power through you.

—ADRIAN BEALE, Co-author *The Divinity Code to understanding your dreams and visions* & Author of *Hidden in Plain Sight*

Alex Parkinson's new book "Partakers of the Divine" is a brilliant read and a must for all who are hungry for the deep things of God. I've known Alex and Jordan for many years now and both are graduates of the Kingdom Life Institute in Murfreesboro, Tennessee. I've watched Alex go after the supernatural endowments of the Divine nature and know that he's found a place in God that has inspired many. Alex is a miracle worker and great revelatory teacher and communicator that has masterfully articulated a blueprint into the supernatural. I highly recommend this book as a mandatory read!

—JEFF JANSEN, Global Fire Ministry International. Senior Leader at Global Fire Church. Author of *Glory Rising, Furious Sound of Glory, Enthroned*

This is Alex Parkinson's manifesto; a prophetic document that will help you evaluate and prioritize your own supernatural core values. Get ready to not just observe the possibilities but to actually partake of the divine character, nature, power, and glory of God.

—DARREN STOTT, Lead Pastor at Seattle Revival Center

Alex Parkinson is an emerging prophetic voice, miracle worker, Revivalist and this new book will ignite both a passion for revelation and understanding. This book will also help you understand how to manifest miracles and truly carry the likeness of Christ as you understand union with Jesus!

—TODD BENTLEY, Apostle & Evangelist at Fresh Fire Ministries

Alex Parkinson's book, Partakers of the Divine is filled with fresh revelation from God's throne. I've heard it said, "Heaven and hell are asking the same question: who do you think you are?" Alex Parkinson does a great job of explaining exactly that, you are a Partaker of the Divine Nature. This is a great book for believers of all ages. I highly recommend it.

—IVAN ROMAN, Senior Leader of Empowered Life Church. Friend of God Ministries. Author of *Prophets Among Us, The Heart of the Prophetic, Identity Manuel.*

We all have a destiny in God, but in order to walk in it we must know who we are. Alex walks in this truth and God has shown him that the best way to discover who we are in this new creation reality is to discover His Son, to become intimately acquainted with the person of Jesus Christ. Partakes of The Divine is a MUST READ, Alex will take you on a journey to challenge you to be all He has called you to be by making you see that the more you see Him, the more you see your true self in Him so you can partake of the divine and do the greater things that He has called you to do.

—JOE GARCIA, Leader of the Ontario Prophetic Council. Lead Pastor at the River International Church, Hamilton, Ontario – Canada. www.theriverinyou.com

Partakers of the Divine creates such an internal hunger to operate in the miraculous. Alex's journey and his deep passion to know Jesus Christ, the Person, has created a springboard for him to dive into true compassion and see the miraculous wherever he goes.

My heart was stirred reading this, but even more, challenged to press in to know Christ at a deeper level. We have this great opportunity to go on this adventure with God to see miracles become a normal display in the earth. Alex is a miracle worker, but above all he is a true son and lover of God.

—ELIZABETH TIAM-FOOK, Founder of International Young Prophets, Santa Rosa Beach, Florida.

Alex has, by pure revelation of the Holy Spirit and life experience, masterfully crafted what I believe will cause many to take a second glance at the very defining core of experiential Christianity. This could serve as a manifesto, if you will, for the Kingdom of God that can help reshape false mindsets. It is literally one of the best breakdowns I have come across in a while about your true identity in Christ! Enjoy it and become part of the Glory generation God is calling to change the earth for Jesus sake.

—MUNDAY MARTIN, Contagious Love International www.contagiousloveintl.com

CONTENTS

FOREWORD

There I was, eighteen years old, sitting in my cold Bible College dormitory room flipping through the pages of my Bible asking God for a revelation concerning my destiny, my purpose. The question remained, "Who am I?" Everyone around me seemed to have their futures all planned out. I mean my roommate was a preppy Pastor's kid who had been preaching since he was thirteen years old. I was wondering if I had made a massive mistake in answering the call of God upon my life and was contemplating packing my bags to run from God again.

I was nervous, scared and biblically uneducated compared to these other scripture quoting, sermon writing, preaching machines all around me. While I had grown up in church my entire life, I had actually only been saved six months prior. Due to a sketchy past, when I had filled out my application I left out all the overwhelmingly obvious things like the fact that I had not ever read a Bible and I was only clean and sober from drugs the past six months. Yes, that's right, by the world's standards I totally lied to get accepted into this well-known school of higher learning for those wanting to go into ministry.

While my prayer life was full of amazing encounters with God I could never quite shake the image of my past. Don't misunderstand me, I was on fire for the Lord and had left everything to follow Jesus. I had seen the mass exodus of everything and everyone I had cherished growing up, literally all my friends vanished after they discovered I was now a total Jesus freak, but I had yet to discover the new me. All I knew was the man I once was had vanished; and while I felt completely transformed I still looked in the mirror and saw the same crazy-haired, punk rock kid who had been addicted to speed and alcohol trying to find my way in this thing called Christianity. I was on a mission with no blueprints or roadmaps as to where I was headed, just a burning man blazing away seeking Jesus everyday.

I was told weeks into my conversion that I needed to pace myself in God because no one can serve Jesus the way I was and last. In other words, they said, settle down and get into the religious flow of nominal Christianity. I despised the very thought of religion and had made a promise to myself that I would never find myself in a place of hypocrisy or religious tradition. I needed a revelation! It had to go beyond a feeling or even a vision and while all of that is deeply important to the walk of the believer; I desperately needed to discover myself in the word of God. I needed to see a new image of myself, I needed to look into a different mirror!

I prayed the only prayer I really knew, aside from praying in other tongues, "HELP JESUS!" I did something that most preachers would never suggest. I closed my eyes and flipped quickly through the pages, stopping abruptly to point at a passage of scripture all the while praying. I opened my eyes believing for a word from the Lord because I desperately needed one at that moment. Eyes open and finger firmly planted in the middle of two scriptures I read them out loud to myself.

"According as his divine power hath given unto us all things that pertain unto life and godliness, through the knowledge of him that hath called us to glory and virtue: Whereby are given unto us exceeding great and precious promises: that by these ye might be partakers of the divine nature, having escaped the corruption that is in the world through lust." (2 Peter 1:3-4 KJV)

I started to weep as I read the words penned by the great Apostle Peter through the prophetic power of the Holy Spirit, for it was Peter who also said, "We have also a more sure word of prophecy; whereunto ye do well that ye take heed, as unto a light that shineth in a dark place, until the day dawn, and the day star arise in your hearts: Knowing this first, that no prophecy of the scripture is of any private interpretation. For the prophecy came not in old time by the will of man: but holy men of God spake as they were moved by the Holy Ghost." (2 Peter 1:19-21 KJV) I had found a transformational passage, a God inspired prophetic promise that upon study — marked me as a changed man, "partakers of the divine nature". I felt as though I was instantly baptized in the presence of God. The weight of this revelation hit my spirit and all I could shout was, "YES!". This is who I am, a Partaker of the Divine.

At first it sounded too grand to believe. God was giving me a life marked by the very nature of God. He was giving me a God-Life! A chance to leave my past behind and embrace a new nature that was naturally supernatural. A call to preach, yes; but greater yet, a call to be a son of God. For nearly three years I saw it everywhere in the

Scriptures on every page I looked. The Father had given us an invitation to live out of the divine abundance of Jesus.

The book you are holding in your hand is not by chance, for I believe nothing is by chance. That day that I flipped through the Bible and landed on 2 Peter 1:3-4 was not an accident, it was divine provocation. It was a revelation that God had destined to work into me. He wanted to give me another image, a new mirror. I had to search for years to discover the Truth, but for you the answer is in your hands. You didn't pick this book up by accident and flip to the forward to see if it would be a good idea to read it, no it was provocation. This is your moment to grow and be changed, for in the pages of this book you will discover a treasure trove of revelation tirelessly worked out by a man who I personally know lives this message everyday.

For Alex Parkinson, this is not a subject, this is a divine revelation that he partakes of daily. Seeded through life experiences as well as Scriptural references, Alex takes you on a journey into the divine nature of God that belongs to you. This book will give you everything that you need to be a partaker of the divine. The seeds of revelation revealed will be implanted into your spirit to root you in your identity, never to return to mediocre Christianity. I pray as you read this powerful book that you will receive the same baptism of the divine that I received during those years of study. You are not who you once were, enjoy the journey, friends.

—PROPHET CHARLIE SHAMP, Founder,

Destiny Encounters International, Author of

Mystical Prayer

L et's start from the beginning. And no, I don't mean in Genesis chapter one. I mean your new beginning. If you haven't heard already, there was a miracle that took place when you first believed in Christ; something supernatural. You may not realize it yet, but deep within the unseen fabric of your being a regeneration occurred; a re-creation if you will. This re-creation is called the new creation reality.

> Therefore if anyone is in Christ, he is a new creature; the old things passed away; behold, new things have come (2 Cor 5:17 NASB).

What if I told you that you're not who you used to be? That in Christ, you are actually far greater and more powerful than you even realize?

For many this idea is thought provoking and challenging. But I want to explain that this greatness I speak of isn't of ourselves, but rather a Divine grace given freely by God.

We are new creatures in Christ. We're not just better people because of Jesus, nor are we modified versions of our old self. A new creation account has taken place; a new genesis if you will. We are new altogether and made to become partakers of the Divine nature (2 Pet 1:4).

This is the foundational crux of Christianity, yet one of the greatest of mysteries; that by the perfect work of Christ on the cross we have entered into a new and living way that restores our relationship with God and transforms our being.

We have been loosed from the dominion of sin and death, having had the adamic contract canceled and made of no effect in our lives. We have shifted from darkness to light and have been given a new nature that isn't prone to sin, but prone to righteousness, as well as a Kingdom mandate that calls us to manifest heaven on earth.

God is breathing revelation toward this matter, because His Body has been confused in their identity for too long. We're unable to take our place of dominion in the earth because we still behave as if we're sinful, unchanged people. Yet Christ died a brutal death, becoming sin so that we could become the righteousness of God in Christ (2 Cor 5:21).

This book is about waking up to our new nature. I want to explore all of the realms of possibilities in Christ, recognizing that all things are possible for them who believe (Mark 9:23), as well as give valuable keys to unlock your true calling.

There are intimate dimensions of relationship with God; pathways that, when discovered, will shape and transform our lives. This in turn, will align us with our destiny. I once heard the Lord say to me "intimacy with Me will unveil your identity. Identity will cultivate your prophetic destiny." So this book in a nutshell, will serve you in these three areas: intimacy, identity, and destiny.

We all have a destiny in God, but in order to walk in congruence with that destiny we must know who we are. God has shown me that the best way to discover who we are in this new creation reality is to discover His Son; to become intimately acquainted with the person of Jesus Christ. The more we see Him, the more we see our true self in Him.

But we all, with unveiled face, beholding as in a mirror the glory of the Lord, are being transformed into the same image from glory to glory, just as from the Lord, the Spirit (2 Cor 3:18).

We are people of power and glory who are grabbing ahold of our destiny scroll, and not just for ourselves, but for cities, regions, states and nations! God is healing our land through a body of people who have tapped into His Divine nature. It is my prayer that as you read this book God would stir within you a holy hunger and zeal for His ways, and that you would find yourself walking in a true revelation of Jesus Christ.

CHAPTER ONE

THE ASCENDED LIFE

"If I find in myself desires which nothing in this world can satisfy, the only logical explanation is that I was made for another world."

—-C.S. Lewis

Identity has become a powerful message amongst today's culture. People are grasping the truth that we are the manifestation of who we believe ourselves to be. Society is confirming what scripture has said, that as a man thinks in his heart, so is he (Prov. 23:7).

So who are you? Who do you believe you are? And why?

We must all ask this question. I've found that we grow up to form self-made identities based on things such as our culture, religious upbringing, economic status, race, etc. but mainly we identify with what we've done, what we do and how well we do it. We identify with actions.

I grew up skateboarding. At 12 years old my twin brother and I began skating every day, all day. Skating was our life. And for me (I can't speak for my brother) it was something I took pride in because it was finally a "sport" I could do.

See, a vital part of my story is that my brother and I were born visually impaired by a rare eye disease. This made it difficult for us to play traditional sports such as basketball, baseball or football. In school I would try my hardest to play these games but I simply could not see the ball. This became something that depressed me because I wanted to be a "normal" kid who could have fun with the rest of the kids.

Skateboarding is something my eyesight can handle somehow. I don't have to catch or throw anything. The board is right under me. It's great! So my brother and I got hooked on skating and learning tricks and progressed very quickly!

By our late teens many considered my brother and I "the best in town." We even picked up local sponsors. I thought for sure I was going to spend my life skateboarding and intended on becoming a professional.

I thought, "Finally! Something I'm good at." What soon happened was that I began to form my identity around skateboarding. It became my barometer of how "good" I was. I felt the high of being seen, accepted and respected for my skill. Therefore, any time I would fail I would take it personally, as if I were a failure.

With skateboarding as my example, I was only as good as the tricks I could land and the people I impressed because my identity was wrapped up in my performance.

The same applies to us all. We gain our self-worth by how well we do our jobs, how wealthy we are, whether we come from a nice family or not, etc.

In the Christian realm, it's easy to believe we gain worth by performing religious tasks. We work to do righteous things, which we ought to practice, but what's wrong is when this gets the privilege of defining who we are.

I want to remind you; your identity is a heavenly identity. You are not defined by what you can do or by what you've done.

You are not your sin. You are not your mistakes. You may have failed, but you're not a failure. You may think you've ruined your life but that will never remove your intrinsic value.

You are not your addiction or your bad habit. You are not your handicap or disability. You are not your personality or temperament either!

You are also not your righteousness. You are not your success. You are not your blessings. Although these are wonderful, do they really change who you are?

The truth is, we are defined by who Christ is and what He has done. This means on our worst day we are in Christ alone, and on our best day it is Christ alone.

One way I see the Gospel is that Jesus has become what man was so that man could become what He is. He became sin on the cross, so that we could become righteous. He was beaten and crushed, so that we could embrace healing. He was separated temporarily by God, crying out "My Father, My Father. Why have You forsaken Me?" So that we would never have to cry that cry of separation from God ever again!

We know that we have been crucified with Christ (Gal 2:20), and we know that if we have died with Him, we will also live with Him (2 Tim 2:11). But now we are seeing that we have ascended with Christ and are now seated with Him in heavenly spheres (Eph 2:6). This means that because we are in Christ, we rule and reign with Him in heavenly places. This makes our identity a heavenly identity, not just an earthly one that can change and fail.

There are innumerable truths to be discovered with this revelation. Here in this chapter I want to dive deeper into the ascended life to examine some of the realities we enter by faith.

AS HE IS

Colossians chapter one brings an important truth to the table. That Christ is "...the expressed image of the invisible God, the firstborn amongst all creation (Col 1:15)."

There are two things we need to see. First, Christ is the exact image of God, The Father. This is later confirmed in Hebrews 1:3, that He is the express image of God's glory.

Jesus Himself said that if you've seen Him, you've seen The Father. A statement to show that He and the Father are one in Spirit and that if we want to know who the Father is and what He is like, we can find all of Him in His Son, Jesus.

Jesus came to put a face on God. He came to show exactly who God is.

However, we must also see the latter half of this verse. That Christ is also the firstborn of all creation (also see Rom 8:29). This means that Christ not only perfectly represents who God is; as a firstborn Son of many, He also perfectly models what it looks like to be a person living in the new creation.

In other words, Jesus came as The Original Son of God, died in our sinful place, so that we could enter into His Sonship with The Father.

In doing so, He demonstrated to the world what it looked like to be a man living under the Divine nature. With Jesus we see a man who was a human like us, yet more than human.

I'm going to tell you now. If you are in Christ, you too are more than human!

You are a son of glory, just as He is. You are righteous as He is Righteous and holy as He is Holy. It brings The Father great glory to recognize this. We have thought that it might rob God of His glory, but God delights in bringing us into union with Himself and all that He is!

> Jesus prayed, "The glory which You have given Me I have given to them, that they may be one, just as We are One (John 17:22)."

Christ has lifted us into royal dignity with Himself. He has brought us up to sit next to Him, and spiritually speaking, that is where we are now. The Bible states that "as He is, so are we in this world (1 John 4:17)."

Have you thought about this? It doesn't say as He was, but as He is right now in His seat of glory and splendor. That's how we are in this world.

THE KINGDOM REALM

Heaven is a Kingdom Realm that exists within the believer. For too long we've *only* thought of Heaven to be a place far away. Jesus challenged this way of thinking in saying the Kingdom of God is at hand, which means it is present and up close and personal.

Heaven isn't a destination, it is a reality. I like to call heaven a hyper reality, because it is more real than real can be expressed. It's a realm of kingship and glory far beyond words.

The word realm is defined to be a kingdom or a government. Jesus carried this governmental realm of The Kingdom on His shoulders as He walked the earth.

"For to us a Child shall be born, to us a Son shall be given; And the government shall be upon His shoulder, And His name shall be called Wonderful Counselor, Mighty God, Everlasting Father, Prince of Peace." Isaiah 9:6 AMP

Jesus' Headship is His Kingdom, and we read in the gospel of Luke that the Son of Man had no place to lay His head (Luke 9:58). This wasn't alluding to the idea that Jesus was homeless (He wasn't). It was pointing to the fact that Jesus was looking for a body or a place He could rest His Headship. Jesus Christ wants His Kingdom to reign on a body of people.

This is why the Body of Christ is important, because together we carry the dominion of heaven as a royal race. We are earthen vessels who contain the treasure of Christ and His Kingdom within.

This has major implications. A paradigm shift is needed to grasp this truth; that heaven is now in the believer and on the Body of Christ.

This is why the Kingdom of God is within (Luke 17:21), yet the Kingdom comes in our midst. The Holy Spirit is within, yet we pray come Holy Spirit and His anointing comes upon us to touch the lives of all present. In the New Covenant God makes us the temple which He fills with His glory, yet God still fills our services and corporate gatherings with His manifest presence. It is internal and external.

Bill Johnson says, "The Holy Spirit is in me for me, but He's on me for you." God gives us His precious Spirit to live within so that we may become transformed, but I've found that He comes upon us to shake the earth with His power and glory.

Years ago I began to recognize this ascended life I am writing to you now. It was as if the light bulb of revelation turned on in my spirit; that I am more than human just as Christ was more than human while on the earth. God began to lead me to minister to others in my life and I quickly began to see the supernatural demonstrated on a regular basis.

He primarily began using me to pray for the sick. Now this was a challenge in my mind. I'll remind you that I myself need a miracle in my eyesight, so when God asked me, of all people, to begin praying for healing for others I was skeptical as to whether God could actually use me. However, I couldn't shake the fact that the Bible proclaims the prayer of faith will save the sick (James 5:15). I had to ask myself "am I really going to allow my handicap to serve as an excuse to disobey God?"

What I soon discovered was that it doesn't matter at all what I'm personally struggling with in my own health. God is looking for believing believers who will pray faith-filled prayers and decree that sickness, disease and death bow down in Jesus name!

Over the years my wife Jordan and I have witnessed the hand of God heal just about anything you could think of. We've seen people born deaf become instantly healed, cripples walk out of wheelchairs, deadly stages of cancer removed after prayer and so much more.

When all of this started happening I told the Lord that I wanted to pray for as many cases of blindness as He will allow me to pray for! The testimonies since that time are numerous.

One story that comes to mind is when my wife (who was my girlfriend at the time) and I went on a mission trip with a team to Malawi, Africa. We were a part of a gospel crusade with a man of God who was preaching nightly. There were countless miracles including the greatest miracle of all, salvation. We collectively saw 100,000 decisions for Christ during the entire time in Malawi!

One day I was asked to preach in a village of about 500 people. I shared the gospel and many responded to give their lives to Jesus. I then gave an invitation for anyone who was deaf or blind to come to the platform to receive prayer. I was surprised to see a man ushered up who was both blind and deaf!

I'll be honest, I was freaking out inside. I've never prayed for such a condition, but I felt in that moment the gift of faith kick in. All of the sudden I knew it was the day for this man's miracle. I then reasoned that I can pray for his eyes and ears separately. His ears were instantly healed and his first words he repeated were "Hallelujah! I can hear! Thank you Jesus!"

I then reasoned with the crowd that if God opened the man's ears He will open his eyes as well. After praying there came a point where his eyes got very big as he realized his sight was totally restored! This man was very emotional and scared as he was experiencing this all for the first time again in many years. The village began to roar praises toward Jesus for this amazing miracle!

I will devote an entire chapter on the ministry of miracles, signs and wonders. This is merely one aspect of what it looks like to live from above. I can tell you this, every manifestation from heaven, all begins with a revelation of heaven within. Let me explain more.

THE NATURE OF REVELATION

Revelation from God is not the same as knowledge. Knowledge can acquire facts and information, but revelation is a heavenly substance that causes our eyes to see and understand the knowledge we obtain. To know about a matter and to understand a matter are two different things. I believe they have stood separate for a long time, but God wants revelation and knowledge to become married together into revelation knowledge.

We live in an age filled with knowledge about spiritual things, but there's wisdom and revelation from heaven being added to God's people so they can understand and rightly apply what is received.

I could possibly write an entire chapter on the nature of revelation and its power. For now I want to focus on its initial role of revealing and its end result of bearing fruit in our lives.

To make it simple, revelation reveals that which has always existed in God. Similar to pulling the tarp off of a car to reveal what kind of car it is. The car has always been there but now it can be seen, examined and driven.

Real revelation from God always produces fruit. One day I researched the definition of the word revelation and was amazed to find a synonym for the word was manifestation.

I then discovered that this was biblical as well. In Romans chapter eight, we read:

> "For the anxious longing of the creation waits eagerly for the revealing of the sons of God." Romans 8:19 NASB

The word used here for revealing is the Greek word, apokalypsis (Strong's G601) and it is translated as: to lay naked and bare, to disclose truth or instruction, and to appear or manifest.

In other words, revelation and manifestation work hand in hand. What begins as a revelation from God will eventually become a manifestation of God.

This is why we must get a revelation of who we are and who God is. Otherwise we settle for a knowledge of God, which leaves us in unending debate and speculation about who He is and what He's like.

For many years I struggled with anger. I can remember having nasty fits of rage as a young teen. This usually occurred while skateboarding. I loved skating but once again my identity was wrapped up in it. So if I had a bad day it meant I was bad. I would scream, break my board and cause a scene at the skatepark.

As a young believer I knew that God had changed my life and I wanted to now please Him in everything, but I felt like a major hypocrite as I would try to witness to other teens at the skatepark but then five minutes later throw a temper tantrum!

It wasn't until I had a revelation of the new creation reality that I began to see my behavior change. I took time to renew my mind according to my true self, which transformed me in so many ways! Many today would have no clue that I ever struggled with anger because there is simply no trace of the anger anymore.

Holy Spirit wants to breathe revelation so our eyes can see the truth, which will in turn make us free (John 8:32). You will manifest all who Christ is the more you position yourself to receive heavenly revelation of who you are in Him. In the next chapter I want to explore the topic of prayer. I believe this will unveil many truths and serve as a tool to ascend higher in The Lord.

KINGDOM KEY POINTS:

- Your identity is a heavenly identity. If it were earthly it could shift and change based on performance.
- Like Jesus when on the earth, you are human yet more than human.
- The Kingdom of God is both internal and external.
- Revelation produces manifestation.

CHAPTER TWO

REALMS OF PRAYER

*"There are many beautiful things in the world around us,
but pearls can only be discovered in the depths of the sea; if
we wish to possess spiritual pearls we must plunge into the
depths, that is, we must pray. We must sink down into the
secret depths of contemplation and prayer. Then we shall
perceive precious pearls."*
—*Sadhu Sundar Singh*

ntimacy, by definition, is a close familiarity or
friendship. Relationships are about our ability
to choose connection with others, avoiding
disconnection at all costs. God has always desired
connection with us. There was never a moment in
time where He stopped seeking to know us
intimately. I remember years ago I had an
opportunity to travel with a preacher to assist him

for the weekend. I was fairly inexperienced when it came to prayer and the things of God (I'm still learning!). I respected this person a lot and had preconceived ideas about what the trip would look like. I thought I would get to talk with him during the entire drive and maybe get lots of opportunity to hang out and receive mentorship.

Even though we did have some time to talk, I was amazed at how much of the time this man of God wanted to pray. Almost immediately after beginning our drive he put on this beautiful worship music. I can remember the presence of God sweeping through the car like a fresh wind. As this took place, I began to hear him softly speaking in tongues as he began worshipping in the Spirit. This took place for the majority of the drive.

After arriving to the hotel we had a few hours to kill before the service that night. Once again I thought, "Alright, now it's time for some fun!" I was thinking maybe we'd grab some food or see the city a little, but almost immediately this preacher closed the door to the room we were sharing and began praying in the Spirit yet again. He was turning his heart over to the Lord to seek out what He might have him do that night.

I wasn't used to praying so much and to be quite honest I got bored pretty quick. It was challenging for me to stay engaged let alone awake! I began to feel like a disciple who was falling asleep after Jesus had asked them to watch and pray. For Jesus said, "watch and pray so that you will not fall into temptation. The Spirit is willing, but the flesh is weak. (Matt 26:43)."

I began to quickly learn how willing the Holy Spirit is in our prayer life. Later that night I was amazed at the presence and power of God in the service. There were notable miracles, pin-point accurate prophecies and words of knowledge, but most importantly; the glory-presence of Jesus.

I remember my eyes filling with tears as I correlated these manifestations with the many hours in which this friend of God drew near to receive such grace. It opened my eyes and put a hunger in me to know Holy Spirit the way he did. Ever since this time I've committed myself to learning the ways of God.

> The Bible says, "But the one who joins himself to the Lord is one spirit with Him.' (1 Cor 6:17)

In this chapter I want to talk about communing with Holy Spirit in prayer on a spirit-to-spirit basis. I want to explore friendship with God and what it looks like to abide in the secret place.

Before I go more in depth with prayer, I feel it's important to discuss Holy Spirit's role in our lives today. I've found three Greek words that I believe help us to understand our relationship with Him.

PARAKLETOS

Why is there such an emphasis on Holy Spirit? Jesus said to the disciples, "It is to your advantage I go away; for if I do not go away, the Helper will not come to you; but if I depart, I will send Him to you," (John 16:7).

The Helper is Holy Spirit. You see, Jesus is seated in glory at the Father's right hand. His Spirit however is with those who believe on earth. It's important to recognize that Holy Spirit is an equal person within the Godhead. Holy Spirit is God, yet the function of Holy Spirit is different than the function of Jesus and the function of the Father. All three are one in purpose and desire but carry unique operations toward us individually.

I love the word helper. In the Greek language it is parakletos, and it has a sevenfold meaning. Holy Spirit is our Helper, Comforter, Counselor, Intercessor, Advocate, Strengthener, and Standby.

> "And I will ask the Father, and He will give you another Comforter (Counselor, Helper, Intercessor, Advocate, Strengthener, and Standby), that He may remain with you forever." John 14:16 AMP

Have you ever wondered what it would be like to walk with Jesus on the earth? Well, Jesus is saying "I'm leaving, but I'm not abandoning you. I'm going to give the world My Holy Spirit." Jesus doesn't just walk with us now because He lives within those who believe. He remains with us forever! And it is by His Spirit that this is possible.

Holy Spirit bears witness with our spirits that we are children of God (Romans 8:16), He teaches us and brings to remembrance the things Jesus said (John 14:28), and leads and guides us into all truth (John 16:13). He is our helper!

KOINONIA

> "The grace of the Lord Jesus Christ, and the love of God, and the fellowship of the Holy Spirit, be with you all." 2 Cor 13:14 NASB

Koinonia is the Greek word in the passage above for fellowship, communion, association, intimacy, and participation. Paul prayed that we would have such with the Holy Spirit.

Partakers of the Divine are those who have rich communion and fellowship with God. They are lovers of God's presence and people who have given their entire lives to knowing Him.

In a natural sense, we partake of the Lord while taking communion; eating the bread, which is symbolic of the Lord's body, and drinking the wine, which is symbolic of His blood. We take communion in remembrance of the Lord and His crucifixion. However, there is a deep level of intimacy and communion with Christ in the realm of the spirit by means of koinonia. We can engage with Christ in a very literal way by recognizing what He accomplished on the cross. He made a way for us to draw near to the Father and to enter Heaven as citizens. The access to God is unlimited!

This fellowship with Holy Spirit is a partnership that shapes the Body of Christ from the inside-out. Inwardly, we are united with God in a supernatural way. Outwardly, we are united with our brothers and sisters in a supernatural way. Koinonia creates a spirit of unity amongst the Body of Christ, which makes way for great synergy, love and teamwork to take place. When the corporate church ascends together in prayer and fellowship with Christ, there is nothing that can stop it. All things become possible because the power of agreement has multiplied.

"They were continually devoting themselves to the apostles' teaching and to fellowship, to the breaking of bread and to prayer. Everyone kept feeling a sense of awe; and many wonders and signs were taking place through the apostles. And all those who had believed were together and had all things in common; and they began selling their property and possessions and were sharing them with all, as anyone might have need. Day by day continuing with one mind in the temple, and breaking bread from house to house, they were taking their meals together with gladness and sincerity of heart, praising God and having favor with all the people. And the Lord was adding to their number day by day those who were being saved." Acts 2:42-47 NASB

PERICHORESIS: THE DIVINE DANCE

There's an ancient Greek word that was employed by some of the early church fathers, a few centuries after Christ' death, to describe the nature of the trinity. This word is perichoresis. Peri meaning "around" and choreia translating to "dance." Together, the word is translated to describe God's omnipresence as well as to paint a picture of the relationship between Father, Son and Holy Spirit as a Divine dance within Himself. This word isn't in our Bibles, yet embodies the unity and synchronization between the Godhead; perfect connection, perfect fellowship and perfect love.

What's incredible about this bond is that we're involved. Being in Christ, we stand in the middle of the harmony that exists in the trinity. By faith, we are grafted into Christ, and therefore into the Father. To give an example scripturally, Paul wrote in Colossians 3:3-4 that "...your life is now hidden with Christ in God. When Christ, who is our life is revealed, then you also will be revealed with Him in glory." Can you see how close we really are to God? We are hidden within Him. Paul said that it is our life. That means we now share life with Christ. It is in Christ we live and move and have our being (Acts 17:38). We are with Him and in Him, and He is with us and in us! This raises the question; what if our problem with connecting with God isn't because we're not close enough? Everyone wants to get closer to God, but what I think we really mean when we say that is we want to know Him more. What if He's not far from us? What if the problem is our ability to be aware of how close He already is? I believe effective prayer begins when we recognize that we're in. Not by what we've done to earn it but "by His grace we have received access to the faith in which we stand (Romans 5:2)." I am in Christ. Christ is in me. For those who are in Christ begin their praying in heavenly places. They pray from heaven to earth, no longer from earth to heaven. Because we've been made one with Him, that is where we begin.

THE APPLICATION OF THE HEART

Madame Guyon, a French mystic, wrote that "prayer is the application of the heart toward God."

I used to believe that prayer was about the words I say and the things I do. I thought when I prayed I needed to pray my best prayers, articulating what I say as clearly as possible, and doing so in a fashion that seemed holy. I'd kneel down by the bed and off I'd go, rattling off my petitions and requests. I would talk to God until I felt He heard my cry, then I'd get up, leave the room, and call that prayer.

What I did is similar to what many in the world do. We've been taught that prayer is only vocal or external, and never an inward experience. We've somewhat narrowed prayer down to merely talking to God, yet I believe prayer is more about a heart to heart exchange with God. Prayer is the language of the heart. I see the external things we say and experience as simply an overflow of what the heart is saying and experiencing. The heart is man's greatest priority and largest of responsibilities. We are to guard it with all diligence, for from it flows the springs of life (Proverbs 4:23). It's out of the abundance of the heart that the mouth speaks (Luke 6:45). It's our hearts that prove where our treasures lay, and the fountain in which rivers of living water will flow. You may say, "when I pray, I don't know what to say." Or "when I pray, I don't feel anything." Well good! You're off to a good start then! Why? Because "feelings" begin within the heart and manifest on the body. And words bubble up out of our mouths as a result of the internal love, joy and peace we sense.

It is the internal that creates the external. The unseen which forms the seen. This is where the real prayer takes place. Not to say that speaking to God or asking from God is wrong. We should never think that! However, the realm of asking is merely the first stage of prayer. In fact, I've found there are three realms of prayer.

ASKING, SEEKING, KNOCKING

So before I begin, please know my aim is simplicity not methodology. My heart is to demystify something that at times can be very complex. When venturing into the depths of God, old paradigms are challenged and we become stretched in several directions. So for the sake of simplicity I'll show you three biblical realms of prayer. The realm of asking, seeking and knocking.

Jesus said, "so everyone who keeps on asking receives, and he who keeps on seeking finds, and to him who keeps on knocking the door will be opened (Matt 7:8 AMP)." He said this to make a blanket statement that our Father in heaven knows how to give good gifts to those who ask Him. We will never be denied or rejected by God when we ask, seek and knock with a sincere heart.

Here is a progression in which our private prayer life starts with asking, yet has the potential to transition into deeper states of seeking and knocking. I like to compare this to the outer courts, inner courts and Holy of Holies.

When it comes to asking, we must see that it is a very powerful realm of prayer that can result in receiving many blessings, breakthroughs and answers. After all, those who ask receive! It is a vocal realm where we externally process our needs and desires before God. This realm includes petitions, supplications, travails, speaking in tongues, intercession, etc. It's a place where the Kingdom of heaven responds and a place where God manifests the riches and glory found there.

However, this is simply the outer court when it comes to relationship with God. We can see many wonderful results such as financial provision or perhaps miracles, signs and wonders and yet never truly know God or press beyond the earth realm, into the inner courts of prayer. So there's nothing wrong with asking, but we must know that asking and receiving doesn't equate to intimacy. And what I've noticed is, we will begin praying to God, usually by going through our list of prayer requests, and as time goes by we will feel the "shift" whether it be weariness or a sense of completion.

This is where we stop too soon. The "shift" we feel while praying may be a sense of completion, but I believe in most cases it's actually an invitation to now go higher. Instead of leaving our prayer closets when we feel Holy Spirit, we should press in and continue to abide in God. It's easy to become too rushed and impatient. We must learn to take our time to engage with God, even if it requires a lot in our schedule. Let me share an example from Philippians chapter 4:6-8:

> Be anxious in nothing, but in everything by prayer and supplication with thanksgiving let your requests be made known to God. And the peace of God, which surpasses all comprehension, will guard your hearts and your minds in Christ Jesus. Finally, brethren, whatever is true, whatever is honorable, whatever is right, whatever is pure, whatever is lovely, whatever is of good repute, if there is

any excellence and if anything worthy of praise, dwell on these things.

Notice the Apostle Paul writes that in everything we should pray and offer supplication with thanksgiving, and then we are to dwell on righteous things. This word dwell means to ponder or to meditate. This sounds a lot like when Paul instructed us to set our minds on that which is above, where Christ is, seated at the right hand of God (Col 3:1). What's happened here is a shift from making our requests known to God to seeking and dwelling on heavenly things.

Unlike the asking realm, the realm of seeking involves little verbal communication. We've now transitioned into a place of contemplation, where we still ourselves to wait and simply seek Jesus.

Now we're no longer on the outside looking in. We're in the inner courts of communion and fellowship with God; a place of seeing and knowing. Those who seek shall find. Here, we will have an influx of spontaneous revelation. We may experience things such as visions, dreams, trances, and the inner audible/audible voice of God speaking to us. We become aware of Jesus and the holy presence that surrounds Him, as well as the supernatural realm altogether. Really, the realm of seeking is an intimate place filled with ecstatic experiences with God.

I've had many wonderful times in prayer where I've been "lost' in the presence of God. Sometimes for hours I will rest in the secret place, discovering God more each time, and experiencing dimensions of the wonderful Kingdom we've been translated into.

> But seek first His Kingdom and His righteousness and all these things will be added to you. (Matt 6:33 NASB)

> ...He is a rewarder of those who seek Him. (Heb 11:6 NASB)

God promises rewards to those who diligently seek after Him. Not just material, but spiritual rewards; revelation, wisdom and insight into God's Kingdom.

We must keep in mind the context for Hebrews 11:6 is Enoch. In verse five we read that by faith Enoch was taken up so that he would not taste death; and he was not found because God took him up; for he obtained the witness that before his being taken up he pleased God (NASB).

Enoch was translated to heaven, not tasting death because he walked with God as a friend and pleased Him with His faith. This is the kind of seeking God delights in.

Jesus opened the heavens and made a way for us to go through the veil of His flesh. He has restored to us the ancient paths (Jer 6:16) that we may walk with God as He did. These are foundational truths as we ascend higher in prayer.

> I am the door; if anyone enters through me, he will be saved, and will go in and out and find pasture. The thief comes only to steal and kill and destroy, I came that they may have life, and have it abundantly (John 10:9-10 NASB).

I believe Enoch's seeking eventually caused him to step through the door. Jesus said knock and the door shall be opened. We must learn how to go through the door of the Lord, which is Jesus Christ Himself. He calls Himself the way, the truth and the life (John 14:6). By His death He opened a new and living way into heaven. However, it's imperative that we understand that this truth isn't merely reserved for the after life. Life more abundant is here and now. Heaven is here and now. We may go in and out of the door and find pasture.

There are many examples in scripture of men who crossed over into heavenly dimensions. Men such as the prophet Isaiah who ripped open the heavens and interacted with angels and saw the Lord high and lifted up (Isa 6:1). There are others I should mention who witnessed similar sites. Daniel, Ezekiel and even the Apostle Paul, all had heavenly encounters (Dan 7, Ezek 1, 2 Cor 12:2-6).

One of the greatest examples of someone who entered through the door is found in John the revelator. There are two instances that come to mind from the book of Revelation. The first is from Revelation 3:20.

> Behold, I stand at the door and knock; if anyone hears my voice and opens the door, I will come into him and I will dine with him, and he with me (Rev 3:20 NASB)

Here, John is recording what the Lord is saying to the Church of Laodicea. There's a charge going forth to repent of their lukewarmness (v. 16), and now an invitation is given to open the door for Christ to come in. This is a personal invitation to first let the Lord into our lives. It's important in prayer that we always make room for repentance, opening the door of our hearts for Christ to have fellowship with us. He promises to come into us and then feast with us! Immediately following this passage, in chapter four, we find something outstanding takes place with John.

> After these things I looked, and behold, a door standing open in heaven, and the first voice which I had heard, like the sound of a trumpet speaking with me, said, "come up here, and I will show you what must take place after these things." Immediately I was in the Spirit, and behold a throne was standing in heaven, and One sitting on the throne (Rev 4:1-2 NASB).

Christ is both the door that His sheep enter, as well as the very Shepherd of the sheep. As John walks through the door, which is a portal that immediately ushers him into the Spirit, he sees The

Lord seated on the throne. As he stands on the sea of glass, he witnesses all of the heavenly activity that surrounds the Lord; lights, colors, sounds, twenty four elders, four living creatures, the seven spirits of God, not to mention the glorious worship that's displayed day and night unto King Jesus!

This realm of prayer is the ascended life. The door of the Lord is one that accesses heavenly dimensions and realities. We should earnestly desire and endlessly pursue to knock on this door. For desiring this door is to desire the greatest of things; that we might worship God in the highest possible way.

This glory realm of devotion is one that will transfigure us, and the world we dwell in. You see, we are called to engage heaven that the earth may be transformed. The first reason we pray is that we may draw near to the One who paid it all to have us. The second reason we pray is that God would impart supernatural power to touch the earth. Men have been given access by God to transcend this earthly dimension, that in doing so they may come back down to dwell amongst man.

KINGDOM KEY POINTS:

- Holy Spirit is God on the earth.
- Holy Spirit is our Helper, Comforter, Counselor, Intercessor, Advocate, Strengthener, and Standby (John 14:26).
- Koinonia Fellowship is meant to be both personal and corporate with the Body of Christ.
- The realm of asking is powerful, but doesn't necessarily equate to intimacy.
- We are to seek until we find the door of the Lord.

CHAPTER THREE

DESTINY SCROLLS

"Your eyes have seen my unformed substance; and in Your book were written all the days that were ordained for me, when as yet there were not one of them." Psalm 139:18

The most important thing we can consider is our destiny. In the book of Lamentations, we read that because Israel did not consider her destiny, her collapse was awesome (Lam 1:9). We also know that without vision [word literally means redemptive revelation of God] the people cast off restraint (Prov 29:18).

Without heavenly understanding and prophetic insight toward our future and the destiny of our city, state, and nation, we will live aimlessly and hopelessly bound to what we can only see with our naked eye. We must ask God for a Spirit of

Wisdom and Understanding so the eyes of our heart may be flooded with light; that we may know the hope of our calling (Eph 1:17-18).

I believe when our hearts become illuminated with His light, we begin to see and hear that which is written in eternity. In His light, we see light (Psa 36:9). We begin to peek into the unseen realm where our days were decided before the foundation of the world.

Like the prophet Jeremiah, God knew us before we were formed in our mother's womb, and He "called us to be..." He established our calling before time and wrote it on our destiny scroll.

God, in His love, set apart His best for each one of us. Just like an earthly father might start setting money aside for an inheritance to be given to his future children, God has also predestined His best for all of His children.

"Just as He chose us in Him before the foundation of the world, that we would be holy and blameless before Him. In love He predestined us to adoption as sons through Jesus Christ to Himself, according to the kind intention of His will." (Eph 1:4-5)

God has predestined us according to His foreknowledge (Rom 8:29), meaning simply that God has seen everything contained in time. He sees the beginning, the present and the future. He stands outside of time, giving Him the ability to watch me write this chapter while simultaneously watching Moses part the Red Sea thousands of years ago and the glorious second coming of Christ in our future.

It's vital to understand His predestination is according to foreknowledge. If predestination wasn't in the context of foreknowledge then that would mean we wouldn't have a choice in our destiny. However, God can foresee our future without manipulating our free will to choose. He simply knows that some will choose Him and some won't. He knows that some will embrace what He set apart for them and some will resist it. The choice is ours.

KNOWING THE TIMES AND SEASONS

How do we align ourselves with His perfect will? Can we really see our destiny? I believe the answer to these questions can only be found in the secret place of prayer; the place where we become thoroughly acquainted with who God is and His ways. When we know His ways, we recognize the times and seasons He works in. We see that what worked last time won't work this time, and what happened last season doesn't quite fit into what God is doing in this season. I believe as time goes on we continually enter into new eras, ages, times and seasons. We press upward, ascending from glory to glory.

Our greatest example is the life of Jesus. I especially like reading the gospel of Luke due to the level of detail included within his account. I feel like Luke's gospel reveals Jesus' process of growing up in God. He wrote that "Jesus kept increasing in wisdom and stature, and in favor with God and man (Luke 2:52)." In other words, Jesus was maturing. What's interesting is we read that even Jesus had to gain favor with God.

See, despite what we may think, Jesus wasn't born favored. Nor was He born with power or special privileges. Philippians chapter two explains that He actually stripped Himself of His deity, so that He could humble Himself as a bond servant (Phil 2:5-7). Why? Because if He didn't He wouldn't be fit to be our savior.

He had to come in the likeness of man and live a perfect life in order to stand as our perfect lamb sacrifice, and because of this, He had to learn to live and grow in relationship with the Father while on earth.

Like us, He had to be baptized in the Holy Spirit, learn the scriptures, and be a person given to prayer. In Luke chapter four, Jesus was led into the wilderness to pray, fast, and be tempted by Satan for forty days and nights right after He had just received the baptism of Holy Spirit.

He came out in the power of the Spirit, went into the synagogue and began to read the scroll of the prophet Isaiah. Reading,

"The Spirit of The Lord is upon Me, because He anointed Me to preach the gospel to the poor. He has sent Me to proclaim release to the captives, and recovery to the sight of the blind, to set free those who are oppressed, to proclaim the favorable year of the Lord." (Isa 61:1-2 NASB)

He then closed the scroll and said, "today this scripture has been fulfilled in your hearing (v.24)."

What's happening here? Jesus is stating that what was written on Isaiah's scroll hundreds of years before He was even born is fulfilled through His life in that moment. He was saying, "hey guys, yeah, this starts right now with Me!" He was basically the first living epistle!

Paul wrote to the Corinthians:

"You are our letter, written in our hearts, known and read by all men; being manifested that you are a letter of Christ, cared for by us, written not with ink but with the Spirit of the living God, not on tablets of stone but on tablets of human hearts." 2 Cor 3:2-3 NASB

However, let's not forget what kind of scroll this is. He was reading from a prophetic passage of scripture. This wasn't just a dead piece of historical literature. This was a scroll laced with divine inspiration from heaven regarding the prophetic destiny of Jesus!

You see, before Isaiah's scroll was written concerning our Lord, it was written in eternity on what I call a destiny scroll. Could it be possible that when Isaiah received prophetic revelation that he saw what was written in heaven concerning our Messiah? Do we ever question how the prophets of old got their inspiration?

The prophet Habakkuk saw what God had said (Hab 2:2). How could he see what was said? It indicates that Habakkuk was reading what God would say. He saw what was spoken or written. This is why the Lord instructed him to take what he saw in the vision and inscribe it on tablets (v.3), so that in the appointed time, he would run with what God had said.

I feel it's of great importance to see that contained within all prophecy is destiny, and destiny is something God shapes in the spirit.

When we receive prophetic revelation from Holy Spirit it comes from the unseen realm of heaven. Paul wrote that we look not to that which is seen, but to that which is unseen (2 Cor 4:18). For that which is seen is temporary but that which is unseen is eternal.

Jesus constantly said "the time has come and the time is now" because He understood there are appointed times and seasons where God manifests everything that has been stored up in heaven.

When we continue in Luke chapter four, we find that Jesus began preaching, working in miracles, and casting out demons; things that He had not done until this point in his ministry. I've heard people say, "Jesus never performed a single miracle until He was baptized with the Holy Spirit" and "it wasn't until after His time in the wilderness that He received the power of the Holy Spirit." This is true, but what if we took it a step further to say that it wasn't until Jesus proclaimed everything written on His destiny scroll that He began to see that destiny come to pass? What if the miracles were to confirm His proclamation which states, today I have been anointed to preach, to set the captives free and to open the eyes of the blind?

I believe His time in the wilderness set Him up for alignment with the Father's plan for His life. In

His process of knowing God's heart, He was growing in revelation toward His own calling and the depth of His purpose on the earth. This was solidified in the end of chapter four when He said, "I must preach the Kingdom of God... For I was sent for this purpose (Luke 4:43)." There is a sense of security and confidence in this statement that I am sure is a direct result of His time with God.

When we know God, we know His thoughts toward us and the world. We begin to discern the times and seasons we're in and grow more aware of His course of action for humanity. Just like Jesus, we too can know what's written on our Destiny Scrolls, and we can find ourselves aligned with His perfect plan for us.

A GENERATION THAT KNOWS HIS WAYS

"He made known His ways to Moses, His acts to the sons of Israel." Psalm 103:7

Like Jesus, we must grow to be thoroughly acquainted with God's ways. It's not enough to know His acts. I love miracles, signs and wonders. I believe they're a necessity for every ministry as they bring validation toward the gospel we preach, but I know that God is more than the manifestations and things He does for us. Every time Jesus performed a miracle it was to reveal the nature of His Father and the ways of His Kingdom.

God couldn't do loving things if He wasn't Love. Love is who He is (1 John 4:8). He couldn't do powerful things either unless He is Power (Luke 22:69). God doesn't have to turn the light on when He walks into a room because He is Light (1 John 1:5). God is Jehovah Rapha; the God who heals you (Exod 15:26).

In God's Kingdom, who we are comes before what we do. We are human beings, created to live out of our heavenly identity in Christ. Ephesians 5:1 says, be imitators of God as beloved children; a command that the Apostle Paul would never write unless it were possible. If we are children of God, by genetics we inherit the same DNA as our Father. We are born of God when we become born again.

Even before the new birth in Christ was available, there were men who discovered God's ways. The Lord spoke with Moses face to face as a man speaks with his friend. Enoch was so close with God that he was translated so that he would not taste death (Heb 11:5), but before he left it is said that he had obtained this testimony; he pleased God.

I want my life to please God. I know He loves me, I know I'm righteous and I know I'm His beloved son in whom He is already well pleased, but I want to live that reality. I want to move His heart and bless His name.

My sole desire is to be God's friend. I want to know Him. I want to be so in sync with His ways that they become my ways.

I believe there's a new breed of lovers rising to the scene; people with contagious zeal, passion and hunger for the things of God and a present day move of the Holy Spirit in the earth.

I also believe there's a hurting world who has seen quite the opposite from the church. We've seen forms of godliness that deny the power. Power that neglects character. And spiritually shallow traditions that offer zero help to a world that's desperate for a touch from the God of miracles. I believe we are the change we seek in the earth. Not that the answer lies within us alone, because it will be the power of God in us that shakes and transforms nations. It will be His children who release His Kingdom on the earth. This, however, is only possible when we yield to His ways to get an understanding of His heart. It is knowing the ways of God that releases the acts of God. Moses knew both, but the sons of Israel only knew God for what He could do for them. This generation however will know His nature and because of this, we will witness the greatest glory ever seen.

KINGDOM KEY POINTS:

- We were chosen in Christ before the foundation of the world (Eph 1:4).

- Cities, states, and nations all have prophetic destiny scrolls that must be opened and declared.

- Like Jesus, we are called to go through the process of continually growing in wisdom, stature and favor with both God and man (Luke 2:52).

- The Spirit of Wisdom and Revelation align us with our appointed Kairos timing to know the hope of our calling (Eph 1:18-19).

- God wants us to walk in His ways, not just His acts.

CHAPTER FOUR

COMPASSION: THE VEHICLE FOR THE MIRACULOUS

"The LORD is gracious and full of compassion, Slow to anger and great in mercy. The LORD is good to all, And His tender mercies are over all His works. All Your works shall praise You, O LORD, And Your saints shall bless You.

They shall speak of the glory of Your kingdom, And talk of Your power, To make known to the sons of men His mighty acts, And the glorious majesty of His kingdom. Your kingdom is an everlasting kingdom, And Your dominion endures throughout all generations."

Psalms 145:8-13 NKJV

I wanted to dedicate an entire chapter on the miraculous. There have been hundreds of thousands of books written on subjects such as divine healing and the ministry of miracles, signs and wonders, but I believe my story is unique due to the fact that our ministry is one that has had countless reports of physical healing yet I myself am in need of a miracle in my eyesight.

I know exactly the pain and suffering many handicap people are going through in this life. Even though I am not totally blind and have enough vision to compensate and live independently, I have faced my fair share of struggle, pain and even sheer unbelief toward the idea of an all-loving God. My childhood was full of rejection and embarrassment as I went through school. Never being picked for sports because I was "the blind kid" and always needing help in the classroom. All were things that killed my self-esteem while fueling bitterness and hatred.

I carried this hurt up until I was 19 years old. I had been a Christian at this point for a few years and did love the Lord very much, but I was closing a part of my heart to God, refusing to let Him into my pain. It was as if I wanted to avoid the giant elephant of unbelief in my life. Isn't it crazy how we can be unbelieving believers? We can go to church and dip our toes in the pool of freedom while never diving in.

To make a long story short, I chose to finally dive in one day. I was touched by God in a powerful way while in college. Some friends invited me to a weekend event in Indianapolis to hear a guest minister who carries a strong atmosphere of revival in his meetings. I'll forever see that weekend as a divine appointment. I believe God lead me there to answer a very desperate cry in my heart.

I had been so hungry to know God in a deep way, but was very troubled by years of doubt. Not to mention the pressure I faced while in university to conform to atheism. I needed God to revive me, and God needed me to surrender!

At the end of the service was an invitation to come forward to receive prayer. The preacher approached me and instantly after he laid his hands on me I was struck by the power of God! It was as if His love was surging through me like lightning. I fell down and was shaking for what seemed like hours. While this was happening God was captivating my heart with a knowing of just how loved I truly am by Him. The doubt that contaminated my soul for most of my life was loosed from me and I believe I was delivered of major oppression from the enemy. Thank you Lord!

From that point on I felt different and had a new appetite for The Kingdom. It was in this season of life my perspective on sickness and disease began to shift. I learned that God didn't give me a rare eye disease to teach me a lesson, but I did recognize that my suffering birthed a compassion in me that I knew only the Lord could give, and it is compassion that I'd like to dive into in this chapter.

I never intended to start a miracle ministry. I simply became burdened to pray for the sick. I wanted to see souls saved and lives touched just as I was, but I wasn't totally confident that I could be used by God because of my situation. I remember once telling God, "God, if you'll heal my eyes I'll go into the nations and preach the gospel of The Kingdom as a testimony!" Then God replied back in my heart, "Why don't you start now?"

So I began to read the gospels and I noticed right away that Jesus was a man of miracles. However there was a secret to His supernatural lifestyle and I believe it was compassion.

In many cases we read stories of how Jesus was moved with compassion and this divine mercy became the vehicle for the miraculous. I think something to note here is that Jesus wasn't ever moved by sympathy or empathy. Although these are pure and good, they have served as counterfeits to compassion for too long. Let me explain.

Sympathy says, "I feel your pain, I am so sorry…" Empathy says, "I feel your pain, let me walk with you through this…" But compassion feels the pain of others and then takes action to bring healing and deliverance.

Aren't you glad the Bible doesn't say "God so loved the world that He showed us sympathy?" Sympathy would have left us in our sin and shame, but hey at least God feels our pain and is sorry for us! No, God came into our mess through the form of His Son to rescue us from sin and death. That's a work of His mighty compassion!

The heading text of this chapter in Psalm 145:8 states that God is full of compassion. This Hebrew phrase can actually translate to an overflowing mercy or willingness. God in His overflowing compassion desires to show forth not simply His ability or power, but His tender willingness to heal our situation. I love what F.F. Bosworth wrote in his famous classic Christ the Healer.

"Even during His earthly ministry, our Lord, who is worthy of being adored, would make any sacrifice and suffer even the Curse itself, in order to open the way for His compassion to reach the most unworthy and the most provoking of His enemies. Both the bloody sweat of Gethsemane and the horrible torture of Calvary were but the manifestations of His infinite compassion. He went to Calvary with His face set like flint (see Isa 50:7); for, after He had been betrayed by the kiss of Judas into the hands of His crucifiers, and Peter had cut off the ear of the servant of the high priest, Jesus healed the ear of His enemy, and told Peter to put up His sword. Christ sheathed, as it were His own sword by holding in check the most natural impulse of His holy soul in refusing to pray when, by praying, He could have had, instantly, more than twelve legions of angels to enable Him to escape the agony of the cross (Matt 26:53-54). But then there would have been only a judgment seat, and no mercy seat, for fallen man with all his needs of body, soul, and spirit." (Page 93)

The infinite compassion of God showed through the ministry of Jesus. On several occasions we read the most powerful phrase we could hear from an omnipotent God; "I am willing...(Luke 5:13, Mark 1:41, Matt 8:2)." We are dealing with a God who delivers us from sickness, disease, afflictions and infirmities, not for the sake of proving His power, but because He delights in us (Psalm 18:19).

Have you ever been moved with compassion? It feels different than our own human attempts to comfort and heal. Compassion in and of itself is divine grace that I believe God inspires within us. And when it comes, we are gripped and moved to take action. Part of being a partaker of the divine is being gripped by what grips God.

In John 11, Jesus receives a report that His friend Lazarus is sick, and it's not looking good. What's interesting is the text clearly says that Jesus loves Lazarus yet the news of His sickness didn't move Jesus to action.

> "Now Jesus loved Martha and her sister and Lazarus. So when He heard that he was sick, He then stayed two days longer in the place where He was." John 11:5-6 NASB

Jesus didn't even flinch at the sound of sickness. He stayed two extra days before moving. Why? Because He wasn't moved by needs. This was a man who only did what He saw His Father doing (John 5:19). I believe Jesus was responding to the solution in His heart instead of reacting to the need to pray for His sick friend, Lazarus. Let me tell you, God is not moved by need. There is something else that moves Him. Let's continue:

> "Therefore, when Mary came where Jesus was, she saw Him, and fell at His feet, saying to Him, "Lord, if You had been here, my brother would not have died." When Jesus therefore saw her weeping, and the Jews who came with her also weeping, He was deeply moved in spirit and was troubled, and said, "Where have you laid him?" They said to Him, "Lord, come and see." Jesus wept.

> So Jesus, again being deeply moved within, came to the tomb. Now it was a cave, and a stone was lying against it. Jesus said, "Remove the stone..." John 11:32-35, 38-39 NASB

From this point we know the story results in Lazarus' resurrection. Jesus called him to come out of his tomb, but His voice was not a voice of sympathy but of a voice of One who was moved in His Spirit. If Jesus had only shown sympathy He would have possibly merely mourned with those who mourned and performed Lazarus' funeral, but instead He performed his resurrection.

I want to explain, sympathy and empathy are beautiful but there is something supernatural about God's compassion. It moves us to do what we would never move ourselves to do. This is truly the vehicle of the miraculous.

THE PURPOSE OF MIRACLES

In understanding compassion we gain insight toward the nature of God. God doesn't just do loving things; God is love (1 John 4:8). God doesn't just do powerful things; God is power (Matt 26:64).

One of the most profound things the Lord has said to me was in my earlier years of stepping out to pray for the sick. He said "Alex, the most powerful thing you can do is love... and the most loving thing you could do is walk in My power." This was an eye opener because I began to see that both power and love are inseparable, as well as vital aspects of who God is.

I feel one of the most virtuous things a believer can do is to selflessly lend their faith-filled prayers to the sick and afflicted, because, in doing so, they function in an aspect of God's nature; Jehovah Rapha, The Lord who heals you (Exodus 15:26).

This introduces the primary purpose for the miraculous; it is God's nature to heal. Every other reason is peripheral compared to this central focal point. God loves us and wants us whole.

This answers a variety of theological debate. One of the most popular being cessationism vs. continuationism.

Cessationism is the belief that spiritual gifts, such as speaking in tongues, the gift of prophecy and power gifts, such as the working of miracles (see 1 Cor 12) have ceased with the apostolic age. A continuationist believes the Holy Spirit continues to distribute these gifts to persons other than the original twelve apostles at any given time.

To the cessationist, everything rests upon the shoulders of the twelve apostles. They believe miracles, signs and wonders were exclusively given to the original twelve apostles to confirm the gospel message and seal the Old and New Testament Canon of scripture.

This is far from the truth and I'll explain why:

1. There were men and women who performed miracles that weren't apostles. It is important to see that in the book of Acts there were men like Stephen, who were full of grace and power, and were performing great wonders and signs among the people (Acts 6:8). Stephen, along with Phillip (who we'll address next) were two of seven deacons chosen in Acts 6 to serve food to the widows. These men were not apostles, but had amazing demonstrations of miracles, signs and wonders. Phillip for example was recognized as an evangelist (Acts 21:8) and was said to have preached with

signs and wonders following. "Philip went down to the city of Samaria and began proclaiming Christ to them. The crowds, with one accord, were giving attention to what was said by Philip, as they heard and saw the signs which he was performing. For in the case of many who had unclean spirits, they were coming out of them shouting with a loud voice; and many who had been paralyzed and lame were healed. So there was much rejoicing in that city (Acts 8:5-8). It is clear here that these ordinary men who served as members of the body of Christ were anointed to pray for the sick along with the apostles. This also explains why Jesus gave power and authority to the twelve "over all the demons and to heal diseases (Luke 9:1)," and then sends out 70 more, who weren't apostles, with the same commission. "and heal those in it who are sick, and say to them, 'The kingdom of God has come near to you (Luke 10:9)." We have to remember that apostles are spearheads in the body of Christ. The original twelve carried a mandate to lead and pioneer the gospel in many ways. Based on this fact, it is inaccurate to say that power and authority to pray for the sick was an exclusive right.

2. The Body of Christ hasn't Ceased. How awful would it be for God to leave the body of Christ to fend for itself against the devil? The original twelve apostles may have ceased, but the body of Christ is alive and well. Do you think God wants the body of Jesus to be sick? If the Head isn't sick than the Body shouldn't be either. The Holy Spirit distributes gifts not only to apostles but to members of Christ's body.

The Apostle Paul addresses not fellow apostles, but brethren in his opening statement, "Now concerning spiritual gifts, brethren, I do not want you to be unaware" (1 Cor 12:1). We are not called to be ignorant or unaware when it comes to the operation of spiritual gifts. Cessationism has served to quench the flow of God's Spirit in many lives. It partners with a demonic lie to cripple and blind

The Body of Christ from the truth that Jesus Christ is the same yesterday, today and forever (Heb 13:8).

3. The Nature of God hasn't Changed. Kenneth Hagin once said, "if divine healing isn't for today than God will have to change His name from "I AM" to "I was." The gospel needs to be confirmed with signs following, however this, as I've said, is peripheral vision to the big picture of why God heals those in need. The simple point is that God cannot deny Himself (2 Tim 2:13). Healing and restoration are who God is. If you were to invite God to be Himself what would it look like? He would probably have His way in our lives in a number of ways! God is unchanging and to suggest that spiritual gifts and the operation of miracles have ceased is to suggest that a part of God has ceased.

Jesus has instructed us how to pray in this life. Part of the prayer is Your kingdom come, Your will be done, on earth as it is in heaven (Matt 6:10). This kingdom message has always included healing the sick, raising the dead, cleansing the lepers, and the casting out of demons (Matt 10:7-8). Jesus has demonstrated that it is God's will and nature to heal. His kingdom comes to manifest the rule and reign of His kingship on earth, but His will is the establishment of that kingdom. This means that there will come a day where we will no longer have any more sick people to pray for. As prophesied, "and no resident will say, "I am sick… (Isa 33:24)." It's time we press into God's kingdom for wholeness!

COMPASSION FOR THE MULTITUDES

"Jesus was going through all the cities and villages, teaching in their synagogues and proclaiming the gospel of the kingdom, and healing every kind of disease and every kind of sickness. Seeing the people, He felt compassion for them, because they were distressed and dispirited like sheep without a shepherd.

Then He said to His disciples, "The harvest is plentiful, but the workers are few. Therefore beseech the Lord of the harvest to send out workers into His harvest. Jesus summoned His twelve disciples and gave them authority over unclean spirits, to cast them out, and to heal every kind of disease and every kind of sickness." Matthew 9:35-38,10:1

With the greatest harvest at hand we need to pray more than ever that God thrusts out laborers into the field. However it's important we see that it was the overflowing compassion of Christ that birthed such a prayer.

In the text above Jesus was yet again moved with compassion. This time for multitudes. Previously he had been visiting several cities, preaching and teaching, and healing every kind of disease and every kind of sickness. Then after several days of doing this He sees the multitudes and can't help but feel overwhelmed in His heart. I believe Jesus recognized that He was only one man. He knew that His assignment wasn't simply to populate heaven through His atoning sacrifice, but to multiply Himself on the earth through sons and daughters of God.

It is easy to think God doesn't need us to accomplish His will on earth. Yet God's method, from Old Testament, to New Testament, to now, has always been men and woman willing to respond to His call. The great healing evangelist Oral Roberts once said, "without God, I cannot. Without me, He will not."

The desire that none should perish and that all would be saved, healed and set free from the oppression of the devil moved Jesus to say the harvest is plentiful, but the workers are few. Therefore, beseech the Lord of the harvest to send out workers. This is the context to Matthew 10:1, where Jesus delegates His power and authority to His disciples over every sickness and disease. That delegation came as a result of deep compassion in the heart of God.

We have been given a great privilege in carrying the ministry of reconciliation today (2 Cor 5:18). This ministry is given to those who have become new creations in Christ, or partakers of the divine nature, not merely those who are called as evangelists. For a long time the excuse has been "I'm not an evangelist." Quite frankly, it doesn't matter which office you occupy, when you get a revelation of the never-ending compassion of God for the multitudes you will begin evangelizing! You will be compelled. You will be moved. You will not feel right about "not" offering your hand to the lost.

I used to feel afraid to do outreach and supernatural evangelism. Thank God I went to a ministry school that made it mandatory. I encourage everyone to set aside a season for intentional evangelism at some time. It will change you!

By the time I finished my first year of school I wanted to hit the streets every chance I could. Why? Because God begin to give me a heart for others, and He showed me that the gospel really isn't about me. I tapped into the river of His delights for the world and simply wanted to offer others an encounter with Jesus.

I'll never forget this story of a man who received a creative miracle in his ear. I was in a coffee shop with some friends after evangelizing in the downtown square. We were fired up and although we were taking a break my eyes were open for God's next move.

The Lord highlighted a man reading a book and I pondered how I should approach him. Almost immediately after this thought, the man pauses, puts the book down and makes eye contact with me! He says "hello" and I strike up a conversation with him.

Now, this is where things get interesting. Out of nowhere this man begins to open up his heart to me concerning several personal things- things such as his sexual orientation, drug abuse, etc. The bible says, "regard no man according to the flesh, but according to the Spirit (2 Cor 5:16)." I decided instead of judging him, I would choose to recognize that he's a perfect landing strip for the mercy of God.

I began to lean into God's heart for him. While listening to him I received a quick impression that I knew was a word of knowledge. The word was that the man was a creative writer and that he had gone to school for writing and had even published two books. I thought "well, let's see if this makes sense to him."

You have to understand that many people in the area I was ministering in were into New Age philosophy and spiritualism. Because of this, I had to be wise in how I approached people with prayer. Paul said that he became all things to all people, so that he might win some to the Lord (1 Cor 9:22).

So I ask this man, "has anyone ever read your palm before?" His eyes got really big and he replied, "No, do you do that!? I've always wanted to try!"

I said "No, I don't do that but I like to encourage people in their destiny. Can I do that?" He accepted the invitation and after sharing what I felt God was saying he began to break down in tears as he confirmed that it was all true, so much so, that we moved to a more private place in the coffee shop.

After we prayed and he re-dedicated his life to the Lord we talked for a while. This is where I learned about his ear condition.

This man explained to me that he was born without an eardrum in his right ear. That's right - no eardrum at all! I told him that I couldn't leave without praying for him. I just had a knowing that God would show up!

Now, just so you understand - this man didn't need his ear healed, because there was no eardrum to heal. He needed a creative miracle. A new eardrum.

There was nothing I could humanly do, but compassion for this man was surging through me. I laid my hand on his ear and prayed a short prayer. Once I took my hand off we hear this loud "POP!"

The man began to cause a scene (again) with his tears. Now everyone in the coffee shop is looking at us. He received a creative miracle and was hearing out of that right ear for the first time in his 32 years of life! Praise Jesus! This actually opened up the opportunity to pray for several others and share the gospel.

God wants to display His compassion through us. You may not be called to multitudes, but there is one in front of you on a regular basis. One that is worth the blood of Jesus and someone the Father is overflowing with willingness toward. Will you ask God to grip you with His heart for them?

KINGDOM KEY POINTS:

- God's compassion is more than sympathetic or empathetic. He seeks to heal and restore the situation.

- Connecting with God's compassionate willingness serves as a vehicle to the miraculous.

- There were men and women in the early church who operated in miracles that weren't apostles, thus explaining that the ministry of miracles, signs and wonders have not ceased nor were ever an exclusive ministry to only the original 12 apostles.

- God's nature has and will never cease. He cannot deny Himself (2 Tim 2:13).

- The ministry of reconciliation has been given to those who have become new creatures in Christ, not just evangelists (2 Cor 5:17-18).

CHAPTER FIVE

GOD'S GLORY IN CREATION

"For the earth will be filled with the knowledge of the glory of the Lord, as the waters cover the sea." (Hab 2:14)

God's manifest presence is fascinating many around the world right now. The body of Christ is being swept away in visitations and encounters with God as His realm enters into our earth realm. We are truly living in days of wonder where we are being captivated again with signs of true revival and awakening in the nations. Masses are coming to the Lord, miracles are happening instantaneously, and the kingdoms of this world are becoming the kingdoms of our God. The new is here and it's taking place through a new breed generation of sons and daughters of God.

I believe within every generation God does a new thing (Isa 43:19). We have witnessed amazing demonstrations of revivals, outpourings, renewals and refreshing in times past. Whatever title you want to give it; history has proven that God promises to answer those who hunger and thirst, and we are beginning to see movements where God's glory is revealed.

You might be asking what is the glory? And why do I need knowledge of it? For the sake of simplicity, God's glory is His manifest presence. We understand that God is omnipresent or universally present at all times, but there is something entirely different about His manifest presence. Imagine the atmosphere and environment that surrounds God's throne; the holiness, majesty and wonder that fills heaven. Now imagine that presence visiting you on earth. That is glory! It is when you encounter the true essence of who God is. In 2 Chronicles chapter five the glory of the Lord filled the temple as a result of praise and adoration toward God:

> "...in unison when the trumpeters and the singers were to make themselves heard with one voice to praise and to glorify the LORD, and when they lifted up their voice accompanied by trumpets and cymbals and instruments of music, and when they praised the LORD saying, " He indeed is good for His lovingkindness is everlasting," then the house, the house of the LORD, was filled with a cloud, so that the priests could not stand to minister because of the cloud, for the glory of the LORD filled the house of God (2 Chron 5:13-14 NASB)."

There's something powerful about praise! It is praise and thanksgiving that ushers us through God's gates and courts (Psalm 100:4) and what is seen here is the result of high praise to God; it is holy habitation. It is His manifest presence! Ruth Ward Heflin coined a popular saying that I believe is such a valuable key. She said, "we must praise until the spirit of worship comes, and then worship until the glory comes. Then we stand in the glory."

As Habakkuk 2:14 states, God is releasing knowledge of His glory as it covers the earth. All will know about God's majesty and beauty, and as believers we need to grow to love His weighty presence and ask for knowledge on how to operate in glory atmospheres. We play a crucial role in this as I believe we are actually the New Testament fulfilment of this Old Testament promise. 2 Corinthians 4:6 says,

> "For God, who said, "Let light shine out of darkness," is the One who has shone in our hearts to give us the Light of the knowledge of the glory and majesty of God [clearly revealed] in the face of Christ (AMP)."

Simply put, we are called to radiate God's glory, illuminating it for all of the world to see. In the Old Testament God filled His temple with glory. In the New Testament we become a temple that God fills. As we behold Christ, we are changed and transfigured into His same image from glory to glory (2 Cor 3:18). These are beautiful promises because it illustrates that we were truly made to live in God's presence as a natural habitat. In Adam, all have sinned and fallen short of the glory (Rom 3:23), but through Christ, the access has been restored. We are the generation that Isaiah foresaw when he said, "Arise, shine; for your light has come, and the glory of the Lord has risen upon you. For behold, darkness will cover the earth and deep darkness the peoples; But the Lord will rise upon you and His glory will appear on you (Isa 60:1-2)."

Here we see that even though darkness covers the earth, there is a glory generation that God is coming upon, who will dispel it. "Nations will come to your light, and kings to the brightness of your rising (Isa 60:3)." We are a glorious people who stand in the light of the Lord and manifest His mighty power.

Everything changes under a glory realm. When God floods our lives with His tangible presence it comes to transfigure. In order to understand what this looks like I want to provide helpful keys to unlock deeper understanding of the supernatural.

SEEDING THE ATMOSPHERE

"And He spoke many things to them in parables, saying, "Behold, the sower went out to sow; and as he sowed, some seeds fell beside the road, and the birds came and ate them up. Others fell on the rocky places, where they did not have much soil; and immediately they sprang up, because they had no depth of soil. But when the sun had risen, they were scorched; and because they had no root, they withered away. Others fell among the thorns, and the thorns came up and choked them out. And others fell on the good soil and yielded a crop, some a hundredfold, some sixty, and some thirty. He who has ears, let him hear (Matt 13:1-9)."

In this parable Jesus is speaking about sowing the word, which is the gospel of the kingdom. He is essentially explaining that the word is the same, but the soil is always different. When speaking of good soil, He said it has the potential to yield crops of 30, 60, or even 100 fold.

I see atmospheres like soil. There are atmospheres everywhere in life. There can be positive or negative atmospheres depending on where you are at. For example, funerals have the atmosphere of death, a climate that should never exist anywhere else. Especially not in church!

The church should be a place where heaven dwells and the river of life flows forth. We are called to create atmospheres that serve as good soil for the word to be sown. As a minister, I have experienced atmospheres of doubt and unbelief, fear, manipulation, control, and many more. The good news is that we can change negative atmospheres into heavenly climates by understanding how supernatural realms work.

This is not my original thought, and I wish I could give credit where credit is due, but many have taught in recent years that there are three realms to the supernatural; the realm of faith, the realm of the anointing, and the realm of God's glory.

Sometimes when the atmosphere feels like hard ground, you have to breakthrough by stepping out in the faith realm. Faith carries the ability to open supernatural dimensions. It frees us from the limitations of the natural, elevating us into the supernatural.

As believers we need to always remember that we have been given a measure of faith that the enemy can never take from us. It doesn't matter what setting you are in - God will begin to move when you walk by faith and not by sight. You may see a hopeless situation, but that is when you need to see with the eyes of faith.

It has been my experience that when I start operating in faith God begins to release His anointing. Isaiah 61:1 says, "the Spirit of the Lord God is upon me, because the Lord has anointed me to bring good news to the afflicted…" God's Spirit comes upon us to anoint His servants for the work of ministry. This is when spiritual gifts become activated and operation of things, such as the healing anointing, begin to take effect.

The glory realm, as explained earlier, is God's manifest presence. It is different from the faith realm and the realm of God's anointing in that the glory is sovereign. The timeless realm of God's presence begins to invade and sovereignly ministers to all present. There are limitations on my end as a human. By faith and the anointing I can see 30 fold and 60 fold, but with God's glory there are 100 fold results. I can lay hands on some in faith, and much more under an anointing, but when the glory is present it is God's hand that is touching the people.

It has been my sole desire to live in the glory realm as much as possible. When I minister, I often have a keyboard player assist me in creating a habitation for God to dwell in our midst. But what happens when you don't have someone setting the tone behind you? Jesus didn't have a keyboard player, but yet it said that the power of God was present for healing (Luke 5:17). The answer is we need to create the type of soil we want to sow God's word into. I'll never forget an event I was hosting in the state of Kansas. We were having a miracle service, advertising for all to come who needed a touch from God. That night there was a thick presence. I knew we were in a special place of worship and an atmosphere that was conducive for creative miracles to take place.

When this realm comes you have to begin to partner with God to speak. We read in Genesis chapter 1 that the Spirit of God was moving over the surface of the waters. Then God said let there be light, and there was light (Gen 1:2). When Holy Spirit begins to hover and brood over us, it becomes time to speak God's will.

I began to lead the people to thank God for His presence as I preached my sermon. Part of my message was comparing Genesis chapter 1 with Luke chapter 1, where the angel told Mary that the Holy Spirit would overshadow her (Luke 1:35), causing her to conceive Christ as a virgin. When the Holy Spirit begins to overshadow us the impossible becomes possible.

I soon began to realize my sermon was seeding the atmosphere. God's word was being sown and was soon to be reaped. I had felt like my words carried a little more weight than usual and God was speaking to me about someone in the service who was barren. I knew God's Spirit wanted to overshadow this person just like Mary.

I released this word and a young woman came forward to respond and receive prayer. She explained that she and her husband had been married for three years and they couldn't conceive a child. In fact, doctors had told her that she was barren and would never have children. However, she was in faith and received the word. We partnered with God and asked for a miracle.

Seven months later I returned to this church and this young lady surprised me by showing up with a big baby bump! She and her husband had conceived almost immediately after our meeting at the beginning of the year. They had a beautiful baby that served as a miracle testimony. I believe this was a result of God's word being sown into the good ground of His glory!

PARTAKERS OF THE DIVINE

I believe we are entering the days as promised where the plowmen will overtake the reaper (Isaiah 9:13); a harvest of souls so heavy that our nets will bend and break. It is time we embrace the kingdom mandate to preach the full gospel and shine as signs and wonders in the earth. Get ready for the mountains to drip with new wine and the healing of the nations to spring forth!

There is a rising generation of new breed sons and daughters who are already revealing the knowledge of God's glory. These are kingdom pioneers with a burning assignment to manifest heaven on earth. These people are not bound to this present age because they live from the age to come. I call them tomorrow people because they live in the present but manifest the future. These individuals will blur the boundaries of possibilities, dismantle limitations and will stand as living letters for the world to see. They are mystically united with Christ, unwavering in their heavenly identity and conduits of His mighty compassion. This new generation walks in God's ways and possess the secret things of heaven. They are marked with friendship and branded by furious love. These are Partakers of God's Divine nature.

KINGDOM KEY POINTS:

- We are called to reveal the knowledge of God's glory in the earth (2 Cor 4:6, 2:14).

- There are three realms to the supernatural; the realm of faith, the realm of God's anointing, and the realm of God's glory.

- We have been given a measure of faith (Romans 12:3) that the enemy can never take from us. This makes it always possible to transcend the natural into the supernatural.

- God inhabits praise, and when we praise we invite God's manifest presence to rest upon us.

- YOU are a partaker of God's Divine nature (2 Peter 1:4).

Alex Parkinson is a prophetic Evangelist and Co-founder of Mirror Image Ministries International. Alex has a unique story of being born with a rare eye disease that has led him to a compassionate lifestyle of praying for the sick. He loves to function as a teacher and is passionate about the presence of God, the supernatural, missions and crusade evangelism.

In 2012, Alex met Jordan who later became his wife. Their friendship was one that lasted for many years before deciding to date. In 2016, while on a mission to Malawi, Africa, both Alex and Jordan felt that God was knitting their hearts together, not just for each other, but for world missions and full time ministry. Since their marriage on March 24th, 2017, the Parkinson's have witnessed God's tremendous faithfulness and favor as they travel throughout the nations for the Lord. Their ministry, Mirror Image, was received from a verse in 2 Corinthians 3:18. Which states:

> "But we all, with unveiled face, beholding as in a mirror the glory of the Lord, are being transformed into the same image from glory to glory, just as from the Lord, the Spirit." (2 Corinthians 3:18 NASB)

It is their passion first and foremost to behold the face of Jesus Christ. They believe in doing so we are transformed into His very likeness. God has spoken to Alex and Jordan that if they can get people to just see His glorious face, that He would cause change to take place wherever they go for Him. To contact Alex & Jordan Parkinson please visit their website:

www.mirrorimageintl.com

CHAPTER ONE DISCUSSION QUESTIONS

1) WHAT ARE SOME FALSE IDENTITIES THAT YOU'VE ASSUMED AND HAD TO SHAKE OFF? HOW DID YOU DO SO?

_____
_____
_____
_____
_____
_____

2) WHAT ARE SOME PRACTICAL WAYS THAT YOU CAN RELEASE THE KINGDOM OF HEAVEN IN YOUR DAY TO DAY FUNCTIONING?

_____
_____
_____
_____
_____
_____

3) THE CHAPTER DISCUSSES THE VALUE OF REVELATION AND MANIFESTATION. WHAT AREAS OF YOUR LIFE NEED BOTH REVELATION AND MANIFESTATION?

_____
_____
_____
_____
_____
_____

CHAPTER ONE NOTES

_____
_____
_____
_____
_____
_____

CHAPTER TWO DISCUSSION
QUESTIONS

1) IN WHAT PRACTICAL WAYS CAN THE
HOLY SPIRIT BRING ASSISTANCE AND
HELP TO OUR PRAYER LIVES?

_____
_____
_____
_____
_____
_____

2) IN TERMS OF PRAYER, WHAT DOES
INTIMACY PRODUCE THAT MERELY
ASKING DOES NOT PRODUCE?

_____
_____
_____
_____
_____
_____

3) WHAT DOES YOUR PRAYER LIFE LOOK LIKE? HOW MIGHT IT CHANGE WHEN YOU RECOGNIZE THAT YOU ARE ALREADY "IN"?

_____

_____

_____

_____

_____

_____

CHAPTER TWO NOTES

_____

_____

_____

_____

_____

_____

CHAPTER THREE DISCUSSION QUESTIONS

1) WHAT DOES YOUR LIFE "SCROLL" SAY? WHAT DOES THE SCROLL OF YOUR CITY AND REGION SAY?

_____

_____

_____

_____

_____

_____

2) WHY IS IT SO CRUCIAL THAT WE FAMILIARIZE OURSELVES WITH THE TIMES AND THE SEASONS THAT WE LIVE IN?

_____

_____

_____

_____

_____

3) PAGE 44 MENTIONS HOW JESUS FOUND THE FATHER'S WILL AND AN ESTABLISHED CONFIDENCE AFTER TIME IN THE WILDERNESS. WHAT HAVE "WILDERNESS SEASONS" PRODUCED FOR YOU IN THE PAST?

_____
_____
_____
_____
_____
_____

CHAPTER THREE NOTES

_____
_____
_____
_____
_____
_____

CHAPTER FOUR DISCUSSION QUESTIONS

1) IF COMPASSION IS SO KEY, WHAT STEPS CAN YOU TAKE TO OBTAIN IT AND GROW IN IT?

_____
_____
_____
_____
_____
_____

2) WHAT IMPACT DOES CONTINUATIONISM HAVE ON YOUR LIFE AND MINISTRY?

_____
_____
_____
_____
_____
_____

3) HAVE YOU EVER FEARED OUTREACH AND EVANGELISM? HOW CAN YOU EXCHANGE FEAR FOR BOLDNESS?

_____
_____
_____
_____
_____
_____

CHAPTER FOUR NOTES

_____
_____
_____
_____
_____
_____

CHAPTER FIVE DISCUSSION QUESTIONS

1) HOW HAS THE KNOWLEDGE OF GOD BEEN REVEALED TO YOU AND HOW CAN YOU REVEAL IT TO OTHERS?

_____

_____

_____

_____

_____

_____

2) ARE THERE AREAS OF YOUR LIFE THAT NEED THE ATMOSPHERE OF HEAVEN TO INVADE? HOW SO?

_____

_____

_____

_____

_____

_____

3) WHAT DOES BEING A PARTAKER OF GOD'S DIVINE NATURE MEAN TO YOU? HOW CAN YOU APPLY THESE TRUTHS CONSISTENTLY IN YOUR LIFE?

_____

_____

_____

_____

_____

_____

CHAPTER FIVE NOTES

_____

_____

_____

_____

_____

_____

Pulpit to Page Publishing Co.
USA & Abroad
pulpittopage.com

PULPIT TO PAGE PUBLISHING CO. BOOKS MAY BE

ORDERED THROUGH BOOKSELLERS OR BY

CONTACTING:

**PULPIT TO PAGE PUBLISHING CO. || USA &
ABROAD**

PULPITTOPAGE.COM

Made in the USA
Coppell, TX
15 January 2020